Secrets of ACCURATE PUTTING and CHIPPING

Secrets of

PRENTICE-HALL, INC.

ACCURATE PUTTING and CHIPPING

Phil Galvano

Englewood Cliffs, N. J.

Third printing.............July, 1957

Photographs by

PAUL WING STUDIOS

Putter Designed by

PHIL GALVANO

To the People

Who Have Made This Book Possible:

MY PUPILS

Preface

AFTER A LIFETIME OF study through teaching, I have devised a system that is flexible enough to fit anyone, regardless of height, weight, size, or age.

But first, I want to thank all the professionals and top-ranking amateurs, past and present, whose ideas have contributed to the advancement of golf. For only by putting together their best thoughts and theories have I been able to build this system.

> Practice without science or a system is like a pilot on a ship without a compass. He knows not where he is going.
>
> LEONARDO DA VINCI

I want the reader to understand that I have no more invented these techniques than I have created anything new in golf. I have merely put together the thoughts and experiences of the greatest players in the history of golf. For, actually, no one alive today has contributed anything basically new to the playing or teaching of golf. We must all imitate to a certain extent.

Is there a *correct* way to teach golf? Better still, let me ask this question: Are there any professionals today teaching *incorrectly?* No, there are not.

Let me illustrate. One teacher will say, "Let the left hand dominate in the golfswing." He then proceeds to hit the ball far and straight down the middle. Another pro will say, "No, it's not your left, it's your hips that do the work." He lets go and hits the ball equally as far and as straight. A third will say, "It's not your hips, it's your arms that do the work." He too will perform as well as the other two.

Obviously, all three teachers are correct. But why, then, doesn't the pupil improve more rapidly? The trouble is that, although he is being taught correctly, he is being taught incompletely!

The golfswing is like a string of pearls, and each section of the swing may be represented by a single pearl. Many instructors are stressing their pet sections or pearls. Each pearl has value; but, unless you have the whole string, you have nothing.

Let me explain this relationship still another way. Most of us are familiar with the musical scale. Many years ago, before the scale was originated, each music teacher would proclaim certain sounds correct and would teach these sounds to his pupils. Then along came another teacher, Guido Derezza, who said, "Why should we disagree with one another, each teaching differently? Why not organize the sounds into a basic scale and all work from that scale?" So, the Guido scale was born: Do re mi fa sol la ti do. That is what I have done in golf.

Once you have a plan to work from, improvement is a certainty. Leonardo da Vinci became master of the seven arts because of a thorough system in whatever he did. Do you remember Kipling's six honest serving men who taught him all he knew? Their names are: What and Where, When and How, and Why and Who.

With this system of instruction, there is no doubt that you can become a better performer.

In this book I shall deal only with putting and chipping, for it is in this department of the game that scores can be lowered most rapidly.

Yours for better golf,
PHIL GALVANO

Table of

Contents

TABLE OF CONTENTS

TABLE OF CONTENTS

TABLE OF CONTENTS

TABLE OF CONTENTS

TABLE OF CONTENTS

Secrets of
ACCURATE
PUTTING
and
CHIPPING

Psychology
of

IN GOLF, IN ALL SPORTS, and, in fact, in any physical act, an individual must go through a learning process, no matter how little it may entail. Since this book has a purpose in teaching or instructing in a physical act, it might be well to devote some time to finding exactly what happens to us in this learning process.

Let's get very basic and begin with a simple definition. A skilled physical act, which in-

Learning

cludes the game of golf, is a movement that is done with a minimum of conscious thought. From this we realize that, the more we think about the movements involved in an act, whether it is walking or running or playing golf, the less skill we exhibit. No matter how unathletic we are, there are dozens of actions we perform daily that require physical skill. Consequently, our muscles are coordinated through practice until these skills become automatic reactions.

Walking, for example, is a precise physical act. But if we were to consider where we were going to place our feet or how long a stride we would take each time we walked, our walking would be awkward, ungainly, and erratic. The same thing applies to dancing or to playing any sport.

Violinists and pianists, as well as baseball players and

golfers, must perform their skilled physical acts subconsciously. If any of these people had to concentrate on where to put their fingers for each note or on how to field a ground ball or on the precise movements of their swing, they would be unable to keep up the coordinated motions to which their every movement is attuned. Their bodies respond to subconscious commands from their brains.

And this holds true for all of us. If we were suddenly to become conscious of our movements, if the habits of unconscious movement were disrupted, walkers would stumble; dancers would trip; pianists and violinists would produce weird, unmelodious sounds; ballplayers would make many errors—and golfers would never break par.

To train ourselves to achieve the highest degree of physical skill in the shortest possible time, we must better understand what takes place in the process of learning. For our particular interest, any golfer can take strokes off his score can break par or break 100 by becoming aware of this human learning process—and, then, by making this knowledge work for him.

There is a fixed starting point in human learning called the normal level. And in the normal learning curve there is an initial rapid climb. This is perfectly logical, because anyone who attempts something for the first time is bound to be twice as good as he was before he started. As a person continues to practice in the beginning, his progress is rapid and the curve rises swiftly.

Somewhere along the line, at some point in the learning process, the student begins to progress more slowly and, finally, does not advance at all. This temporary leveling off, which psychologists call the learning "plateau," is the point at which our minds and bodies are integrating and consolidating what they've absorbed and are forming the patterns of muscle skill which are necessary for new achievement. In many instances these plateaus may be of extended duration, during which time we tend to wane somewhat in ability. But by application we can again begin a rapid climb in our learning curve. And, because human beings have different personalities and varying degrees of ability, each person will find that his learning curve will vary from that of the next person. We may reach a number of these plateaus before we are really able to know and master a particular skill.

Can we prevent these leveling-off periods? Yes, to an extent; although they are normal in any learning process. But we are able to minimize the number of plateaus and shorten their duration by following these simple rules:

(1) Present our minds with a complete and thorough understanding of what is to be done,

(2) Train our bodies to perform consciously the act that our minds understand, and then

(3) Perform the act with a minimum of conscious attention.

While you are performing consciously, you will still be relatively unskilled. However, when you can succeed in mentally putting aside everything you have learned, and when you begin to perform your act subconsciously, with your attention away from the particular movements involved, then, and only then, will you experience true physical skill.

As has been said before, each person has a different learning curve, for every individual responds differently to certain stimulations. This is what is known as "reaction time." Let's make this concept more concrete. Suppose you are seated before a button, with a red light directly in front of you, and are given the task of pressing this button as soon as the red light flashes on. The well-coordinated person will react very quickly to the stimulation of the red light; the less-coordinated person will require more time.

The same thing occurs in driving. An automobile pulls out of a concealed road onto a main highway in front of you. One person may react in time to stop his car; another may be able to swerve out of danger onto the shoulder or into another lane. The least-coordinated person, or the person with the slowest reaction time, will be unable to do any of these things quickly enough and will collide with the other vehicle. Reaction time, then, is the length of time it takes you to respond to stimulation. Scientifically speaking, it is the length of time it takes for the brain, upon receiving an impulse, to send a nerve impulse to the muscle whose performance is being requested.

The human nervous system, through which reactions are transmitted, is similar to an electrical system. The auto pulls out on the road; our eyes perceive it; and a current is transmitted to the brain warning of the danger, similar to the blinking of a red light. The brain's alarm system sends signals down the spine to the legs and arms to react by either pressing the foot on the brake or turning the wheel to avoid the collision. This takes place in every individual, for the mere fact that some movement does take place, no matter how slowly, proves that there is a reaction. Fast or slow, everyone has a reaction time; and that means there are no "hopeless" pupils in golf.

How can we then apply this knowledge of the learning process and of reaction time to develop more proficiency in our golf? The most important consideration is intelligent practice, for we know that through conscious effort in practice we can develop the subconscious ability to perform superbly. So we must aim to make putting and chipping as much of an unconscious habit as walking or running. In other words, our job is to speed up the impulse by the repetition of a required action until conscious effort is eliminated and subconscious, automatic response begins to occur.

Remember the reaction time test with the button and light you were asked to imagine before? It has been proven with a series of similar tests that a fast reaction time is one-fifth of a second. Let's apply this to learning golf and assume that you have a reaction time of one-fifth of a second. Here is where the difficulties of golf instruction present themselves.

One instructor will say, "Keep your left arm straight." That takes one-fifth of a second to perform. Another will say, "Keep your head down." Another fifth of a second is used. "Shift the weight to the right foot on the backswing" takes another fifth. So does "Attempt to hit the ball to the right of the fairway to cure your slice." Last week you had a good shot by remembering to keep the right elbow close. One more fifth. You read a book that gave you another suggestion. Again, one-fifth of a second.

In short, since it takes about two-fifths of a second to move a golf club from the top of the backswing to contact with the ball, you're over your reaction time limit if you have the impulse to think of more than two items. The result? General confusion and invariably a flubbed shot.

There is only one way to beat this problem. Understand completely and thoroughly what actions must be performed, on a perfectly conscious basis; and then repeat them, practice them, master them until they can be performed without conscious attention. In that way you can eliminate the unnecessary fifth of a second.

The instructions and suggestions offered on the following pages are devised with these proven theories in mind. The finest golfers in the world accept them, and through diligent practice have made possible the breaking of par.

By learning the correct movements faithfully, with a conscious realization of what they accomplish, and by continuing to practice diligently until they are no longer conscious movements, you can cut many strokes off your game. Remember, while you are learning, and working consciously, you will show very little skill. Again, I repeat, you will have many leveling-off points and falls in your learning curve. Accept these falls, for it is only after you have experienced them that the subconscious truly takes over, and you will experience the pleasure and profit that go with true physical skill.

Importance
of

ON A PAR 72 GOLF course a perfect round of golf normally consists of fifteen tee shots with the driver, three iron shots from the tee on par 3 holes, three shots with woods in the fairway for the long par 5 holes, fifteen iron shots to the green, and thirty-six putts. Of seventy-two strokes, thirty-six, or 50 per cent, are putts. Thus, it is obvious that putting is far and away the most

Putting

important part of the game; and it is here that you can really bring down your score. More tournaments are won or lost because of putting than because of any other part of the game. You can recover from a missed drive or a missed iron shot; but in shooting par you cannot recover the lost putt that should have been sunk.

Keys to a system

GREAT PUTTERS are not born; they are made. Good putting is a matter, not just of practice, but of practice with a system. In building a system there are several key points to understand.

Yards	Par	Hdcp.	Hole	Good Putter	(No. of Putts)	Poor Putter	(No. of Putts)			
DATE		19								
440	4	1	1	5	2P	6	3P			
351	4	15	2	4	1P	4	1P			
400	4	7	3	5	2P	6	3P			
401	4	13	4	4	1P	5	2P			
540	5	3	5	5	1P	6	2P			
220	3	11	6	4	2P	4	2P			
422	4	9	7	5	2P	6	3P			
157	3	17	8	3	2P	3	2P			
478	5	5	9	5	2P	6	3P			
3409	36	OUT		40	15 PUTTS	46	21 PUTTS			
471	5	6	10	5	2P	6	3P			
310	4	14	11	4	1P	4	1P			
360	4	10	12	4	1P	5	2P			
394	4	4	13	5	2P	6	3P			
366	4	12	14	4	1P	5	2P			
405	4	8	15	5	2P	6	3P			
180	3	16	16	3	1P	4	2P			
501	5	2	17	6	2P	6	2P			
120	3	18	18	3	2P	3	2P			
3107	36	IN		39	14 PUTTS	45	20 PUTTS			
6516	72	TOTAL		79	29 PUTTS	91	41 PUTTS			
HANDICAP										
NET SCORE										

Here is the scorecard of two players. From tee to green, both golfers played equally well. The good putter had twenty-nine putts, whereas the poor putter had forty-one putts. One player shoots in the 70's, the other in the 90's. Why? Putting makes the difference.

IMPORTANCE OF PUTTING

(*1*) Which is your "master eye"?

(*2*) What is central fixation?

(*3*) Is your right-angle vision accurate?

(*4*) How can you sharpen your eyesight?

(*5*) What makes the ball spin properly?

(*6*) Where is the "sweet spot" on your putter?

(*7*) What type of putter should you use?

(*8*) What stance will give you the most consistent success?

(*9*) What is the proper grip and why?

(*10*) Where does the energy to stroke the ball come from?

(*11*) How can you judge distances accurately.

(*12*) What is the proper way to read a green.

The Master

THE FIRST STEP IN building your system is to discover which is your *master eye*. Knowing which is your master eye will enable you to line up a putt with greater accuracy.

Select an object in the room, something fairly small, about the size of an ashtray or a pack of cigarettes. Then stand about fifteen feet away from the object. With both eyes open, point at the object with your right forefinger. With your

Eye

finger on the target, close one eye and then the other, and you will notice your finger jumping. The eye that lines up the finger closer to the object is your master eye.

In most cases, a right-handed person's master eye is his right and a left-handed person's master eye is his left.

The eye that keeps your finger on the target is your master eye. It is the master eye, in a human being, which enables his brain to control the muscles that drive a car in a straight line, move his legs in a desired direction, and so forth. It is the master eye that gives the accurate alignment for all acts in which proper direction is needed. Therefore, in lining up your putt to the hole, stand in back of the hole so that you are forming a straight line from your master eye through the ball and to the hole. Line up your putt with your master eye.

Central

WHILE YOUR master eye determines direction, your other eye determines depth or distance. The point where they meet is called the point of *central fixation*. When you look at a photograph or a store window, your brain sees only one image—and that image is clearest only at the point of central fixation.

In order to see the picture or object (that is, the green or the

16

Fixation

flag or the cup) more clearly, you should blink your eyes a few times. Then focus them on various sections of the object you are looking at. In this way your brain receives more mental pictures and your vision becomes clearer. As a result, you will be able to see clearly details that you could not see before. On the green you will be able to see even the slightest slopes and undulations.

When lining up your putt, blink a few times, then focus your eyes on a few spots between the ball and the hole. You will then notice how much clearer the correct line appears.

When striving for direction, favor your master eye; when distance is paramount, favor your depth eye.

Blinking is one of nature's best eye exercises. It is especially

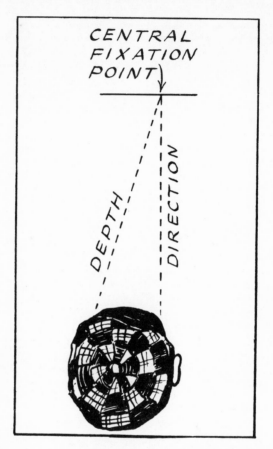

Note that the master eye has a direct line of vision, while the depth eye looks off at an angle which meets at the focal point or point of central fixation.

good for relieving eye strain. (Incidentally, if you do any rifle shooting at a still target, use only your master eye. But, if you shoot at a moving target, use both eyes.)

This takes care of the forward vision. Now let's get down to the right-angle vision.

Right-Angle

L ET'S GIVE OUR EYES the "right-angle" test. This is one of the most difficult of all tasks for the human eye. Most people are off slightly to the right or to the left of their target. Only in rare cases do people have perfect right-angle alignment.

So let us find out how close you are to the correct right-angle vision. Draw a line approximately one yard long on the floor. Then take your putter and place it with the toe of the club at what you think is a per-

Vision

fect right angle to the line. Now, without moving the putter, take a square and place it along the line, snuggling it up to the face of the putter. (See photos on the following pages.) This shows you immediately whether you are in proper alignment. If not, you can tell in which direction you are off. You can then aim to the right or the left of your target, as the case may be, compensating for the degree to which you are off.

Do not worry about not being able to place your putter at a perfect right angle. It is normal not to be able to do so. Most people are off either to the right or to the left. *The trick is to find out in which direction you are off and to allow for this in your putting.*

There is a great feeling of confidence in knowing that your putter blade is in proper alignment with the hole. It makes for increased relaxation so that you can stroke your ball with greater smoothness and confidence.

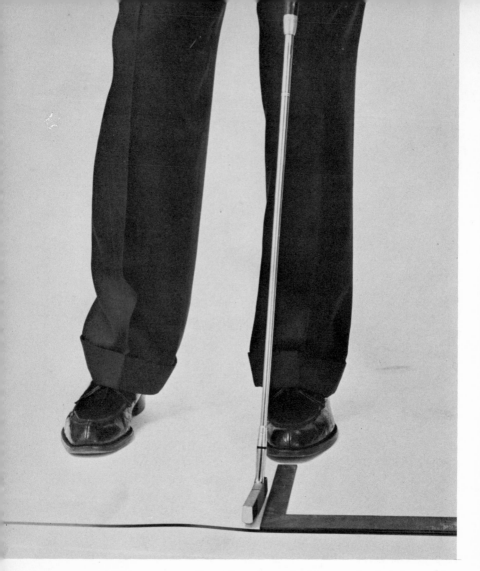

The square, when placed on the line and almost touching the putter blade, clearly shows whether your blade is at a right angle to the intended line.

22

Sharpening

Your

BECAUSE GOOD eyesight is important in improving your golf game, some simple eye exercises might prove beneficial in developing your master eye and your depth eye, as well as in improving your right-angle vision. Let it be understood that I am making no claims to having developed these systems. Nor do I claim that you can throw away your glasses after using these routines.

Eyesight

However, these exercises have been advised and suggested by qualified ophthalmologists to help improve vision and especially to relieve eye strain.

The first four exercises are best done just before you fall asleep; while you can do exercises five, six, and seven at odd moments during the day.

Exercise one

WITHOUT MOVING your head, focus your eyes on the top right-hand corner of your room. Then shift your gaze, without moving your head, to the bottom left-hand corner, diagonally across the room. Shift your gaze from the upper right to the lower left, back and forth, ten times. Then do the shifting exercises for the other corners, from upper left to lower right, in a similar manner. Repeat the exercise until you have focused on each corner ten times.

Exercise two

AS IN EXERCISE ONE, without moving your head, move your eyes slowly from side to side, from the extreme left to the extreme right, along a horizontal plane. Repeat these motions ten times.

Exercise three

ONCE MORE, without moving your head, first focus your eyes up and then focus them as far down as possible. Repeat this exercise ten times.

Exercise four

ROLL YOUR EYES to the left, in a clockwise direction, making a complete revolution of the eyes. Do this for ten repetitions.

Reverse the motion, rolling your eyes in a counterclockwise direction through a complete revolution. Repeat ten times.

Exercise five

EXTEND YOUR HAND, palm towards you, at arm's length. Now focus your eyes on the palm. Shift your gaze to a distant object—perhaps a light fixture on the ceiling or some similar object. Alternate focusing on the palm and on the distant object at least ten times, spending a few seconds on each object.

Exercise six

IMAGINE that a mosquito is crawling across the ceiling or wall. Remembering that the path of this insect may be erratic—sometimes fast, sometimes slow, almost never in a straight line—follow the imaginary trip with your eyes. Then go back to the starting point of the journey and repeat for a total of three trips.

Exercise seven

BLINK YOUR EYES fifty times, with your hands placed over your eyes to eliminate the entry of any possible light.

YOU WILL NOTICE after only one session of these exercises that you are able to use your eyes with a greater degree of accuracy on the golf course. Try to develop the habit of doing these exercises once a week all year around, and you will enjoy much better vision and a pleasant improvement in your game.

Proper
Spin of

THE OBJECT IN putting is to sink the ball as often as you you possibly can. In order to do this, you must give the ball the proper spin. If you strike across the ball from left to right (as in sketch A on page 30), causing it to spin from left to right, it will go true only until it starts to slow down. Then it will curve from left to right. On the other hand, if you strike the ball from right to left

the Ball

(as in sketch B), again it will go true only until the major part of its force is spent. Then it will curve to the left in the same direction of the spin, causing a miss.

In order to keep the ball on line, it must be stroked in a straight line, causing the ball to overspin and thereby eliminating any tendency to curve. Overspin actually causes the ball to hug the green. It is a known fact that a rolling ball will always have overspin. The gravitational pull on a rolling sphere will keep the bottom of the sphere hugging the earth while the top keeps rolling over.

Now, in putts that are stroked across the intended line of flight, you will also have overspin. It is the additional sidespin caused from the cut stroke that causes the ball to curve

29

near the end of its journey, causing you to miss the hole. So, if you can stroke the ball in a manner free from any tendency toward sidespin, you have the perfect stroke. This same principle applies in billiards, ping-pong, and tennis. With the correct overspin, although you may stroke the ball hard enough to go a few feet past the hole, the overspin will tend to curve the ball downward so as to sink the ball if it just touches the lip of the cup.

In order to get the desired overspin, the ball must be played far enough forward so that the ball will be struck after the club passes the bottom of its arc and is on its way up (as in sketch C). That is why we play the ball exactly off the left toe.

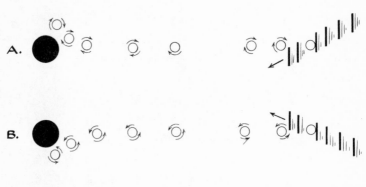

Effect on ball as clubhead strikes ball in the different paths.

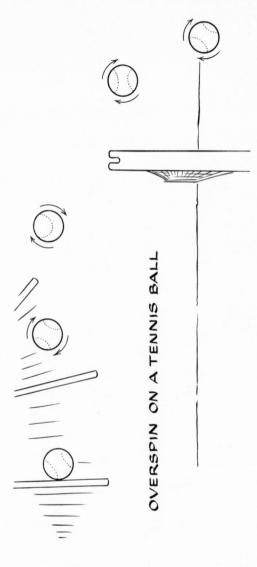

OVERSPIN ON A TENNIS BALL

Overspin on tennis ball caused ball to drop sharply.

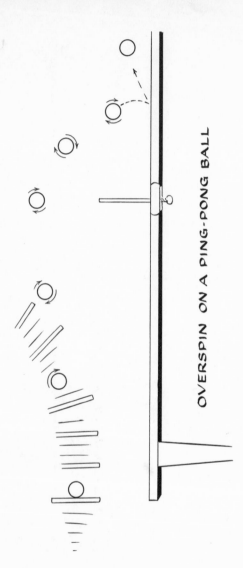

OVERSPIN ON A PING-PONG BALL

Sharp drop on ping-pong ball is also caused by the spin applied.

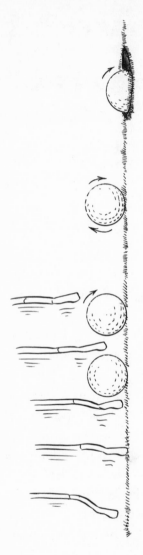

OVERSPIN ON A GOLF BALL
WITH THE CORRECT PUTTING STROKE

Notice that the stroke is rising after contact with ball, thereby eliminating any tendency toward sidespin.

The "Sweet Spot"

ON WHAT PART OF the putter should the ball be struck?" is a question that has bothered quite a few golfers.

Every putter has a "sweet spot." You should discover this spot on your putter. Hold your putter between the thumb and forefinger of your left hand. Then take a coin and tap it along the face of your putter. When you can tap the coin and

on Your Putter

feel no vibration in the fingers holding the club, you have found the "sweet spot." It is this spot that should come in contact with the ball when the ball is struck.

You will find that the "sweet spot" is usually slightly behind the center of your blade. This is the point of the least amount of turn in the putting blade. If you turn your putter blade quickly from left to right, opening and closing the face of the blade, you will notice that the sweet spot on your putter is doing the least amount of turning.

In stroking your putt, see to it that the ball is met in the sweet spot. You will give yourself a better chance for more sinks. Now let's go on to the selection of your putter.

35

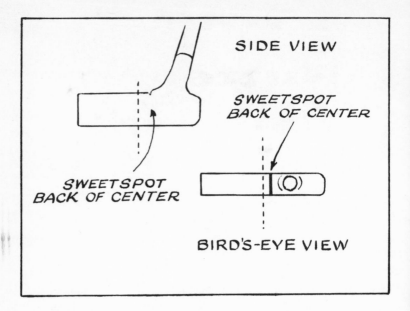

This clearly shows the effect of opening and closing the putter blade.

Tap a coin along face of putter until you reach a spot where you feel no vibration in the thumb and forefinger of the hand holding the club. That spot is the "sweet spot."

Choice of

THERE ARE MANY varieties of putters on the market today and all are good putters and, when used properly, are able to send the ball into the hole repeatedly.

What should you look for in a putter? There are six vitally important features of your putter that you should consider with extreme care: (*1*) length, (*2*) weight, (*3*) shaft, (*4*) grip,

Putters

(5) shape of the head, and (6) placement of the shaft in the head. Let's take them in order.

The proper length

To FIND the proper length you need in your putter, stand with your back up against the wall. Stretch your left hand and arm at shoulder height, with the back of your hand flush against the wall. The distance from the tip of the fingers of your left hand to the middle of your chin designates the length of the putter suitable for you.

Weight of putter

THE WEIGHT of your putter should be between fifteen and eighteen ounces. The closer to fifteen ounces your putter comes, the better it will feel, since a lighter putter will give you a more delicate touch.

Shaft of putter

THE SHAFT should not be too stiff, but should be pliable enough to give you the necessary clubhead "feel."

Grip on your putter

THE GRIP on your putter should have a flat front, so that you not only can see that you are holding your putter straight, but also can feel with your fingers that it is straight.

40

Shape of the head

NOW WE COME to the most important feature of your putter: the shape of its head. There are many sizes and shapes that are popular today. Let's find out which one will give you the greatest advantage.

What do you want your putter to be? You want it to be a tool that will give you a sensitive feel. In addition, you want it to have a head that you can place at a perfect right angle the greatest number of times.

An ideal putter is one similar to the putter diagrammed on page 43. When looking down on such a putter, you can definitely see a right angle, since the top, face, back, and toe are square. This eliminates the necessity of your lining up with just the club face, which has so little loft that it is almost impossible to see a right angle.

Of course, there have been many great players who have used differently shaped putters. But why not make it easier for your eyes by selecting a putter that is perfectly square. It will be much easier to place such a putter at a right angle to your intended line of flight.

Your putter must also have a bottom that is rounded out so as not to stick on the grass of the green when you are stroking the putt.

Placement of shaft in the head

WHERE SHOULD the shaft be in the putter head, center or back? You will find, by opening and closing the putter face, that the farther away you get from the heel of the putter, the greater the degree of error.

The shaft should be placed between the heel and center of the clubhead so as not to lose the very important clubhead feel. This, in turn, will bring the "sweet spot" closer to the shaft, thereby minimizing the possibility of error to such a degree that, although your blade may not be at a perfect right angle to your line of flight, you will still be able to sink that extra putt.

Do not imagine that it is the putter alone that will enable you to keep sinking putts. A person who is a good putter will sink putts with any kind of putter; but precision tools offer a better advantage. A piece of cloth can be cut with a pocket knife; but it can be cut much more easily with a pair of scissors.

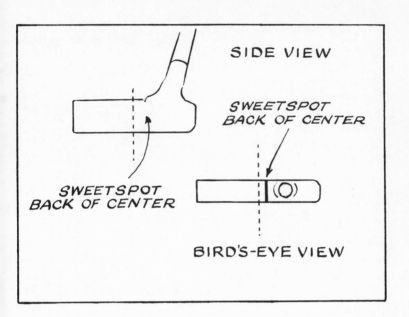

SIDE VIEW

SWEETSPOT
BACK OF CENTER

SWEETSPOT
BACK OF CENTER

BIRD'S-EYE VIEW

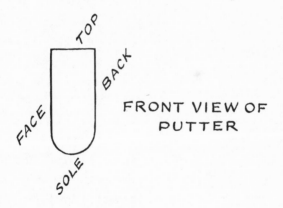

TOP

BACK

FACE

SOLE

FRONT VIEW OF
PUTTER

Putting

THERE IS NOTHING mysterious or complicated about building a proper putting stance. It is simply a matter of placing your feet and body in the proper position in relation to the ball and target.

In order to build a proper putting stance you need a target. Let's not use a putting cup. Let's use a very difficult target: an ordinary straight pin, stuck through a small piece of paper

Stance

so that it can be seen from a distance. Now place your ball approximately six feet from the target. (Do not worry about your putting grip; we will get to that a little later on.)

Using your master eye, form an imaginary line from the pin through the center of the ball. Then place the toe of your putter in back of the ball, cutting the ball in half at a perfect right angle to the imaginary line (as in the first picture in this chapter). This will give you a finer line to work with, rather than one the thickness of the diameter of the ball.

By aiming with the toe of the putter you can also see how far away your left toe should be from the ball. Place your left foot so that your left toe is behind the ball at a perfect

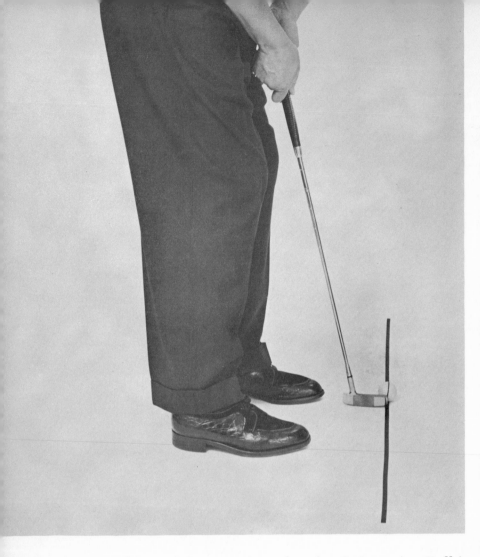

The toe of the putter is used as the aiming point. Ball is close enough to left toe to enable you to keep your eyes directly over ball and weight back on heels.

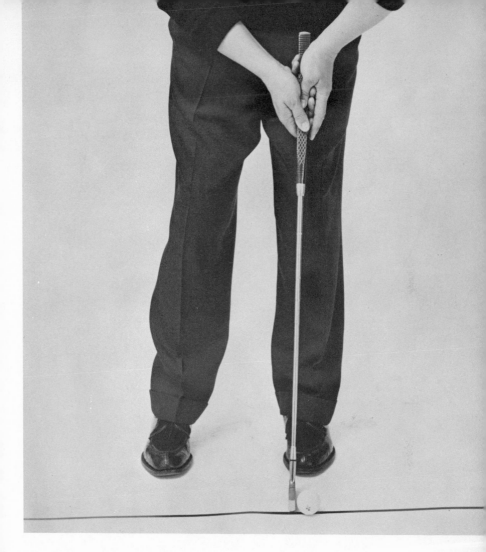

The ball is played off the left toe to allow clubface to meet the ball as the club is rising, creating the desired overspin.

The toes are parallel with the intended line of flight. Eyes are directly over the ball. The right forearm is resting lightly against the right thigh and the left elbow is pointing in line with the toes. Body weight is slightly back and toward the left foot.

*Club is now in position, ready to stroke the ball with the
"sweet spot," which is directly behind the center of the ball.*

As it would appear to a left-handed player.

The correct putting stance. Feet are parallel to the intended line of flight—knees slightly bent to eliminate tension. Body weight on left foot and back toward left heel. Right arm resting lightly on right thigh. Left elbow pointing along line of toes. Eyes directly over ball. During actual stroking, breath is held.

51

right angle to the imaginary line and close enough so that
your eyes are directly over the ball.

Place your right foot parallel to your left. Both toes and
heels should be parallel and far enough apart so that the outer
edge of your feet are the same distance apart as the width of
your hips.

Bend both knees slightly and equally, so that you are in a
squatting position. Bending your knees will relieve nerve tension. The weight of your body should be on the left foot
and toward the heels. This weight position will reduce body
motion to a minimum. If your weight is equally divided,
your heartbeat will make your body move. That is why the
expert rifleman keeps his weight wholly on one foot. Keep
yours on your left foot.

Hold your breath during the putting stroke. This will fur-
ther eliminate body vibration. Of course, don't forget to re-
sume breathing after you finish the stroke.

The distance of the ball from the left toe depends on the
type of build you have. Your eyes should look down at the
ball in a perfectly straight line. That will bring the ball approximately four inches away from your left toe. Very rarely
is it ever farther than five inches away.

Remember, overspin is desirable. By placing the ball off
the toe of your left foot, you automatically get the desired
overspin. The club will be stroking the ball on the upswing,
rather than on the downswing.

Just before stroking the ball, pick your putter blade off the ground very slightly and slide it forward gently and carefully while the blade is still in the air. Slide it forward until the "sweet spot" on your putter is directly in back of the ball. Do not train yourself to slide the blade forward while it is resting on the ground; for, when you are on the green, the grass will make the clubhead stick. This sliding forward will eliminate the nervous tension that is caused by jumping the blade back and forth over the ball as you address it.

Now, let's get to the all-important putting grip so that we can continue to that magic basic putting stroke.

Putting

HOLD THE CLUB with the left hand only, as shown in the first picture in this chapter. Place your left thumb straight down the top of the handle of your putter. If your putter has a round handle, imagine that it is square and place your left thumb on the top of the imaginary square.

If you have long fingers, your putter handle will naturally be in your fingers. If you have

Grip

short fingers, it will naturally be in your palm. There is no set rule for this, inasmuch as no two hands are built exactly alike. The important part is that your left thumb is on the top of the handle.

While holding the club just in the left hand, you will notice that your left elbow is close to your body. In this position you will find that you can easily turn your left wrist and the putter to the left without moving your left arm—causing you to miss to your left. Now bring your left elbow out, so that it is pointing toward the hole or target. Get it way out there! (See the second picture.) With your elbow placed in this position, it is physically impossible for you to hit to the left unless your whole arm turns.

PUTTING GRIP

Now place your right hand on the club with the small finger of your right hand over the forefinger of your left hand. Your right thumb should also point straight down the top of the shaft. Now, by sliding out your left forefinger and placing it on top of the fingers of your right hand (as in the fourth picture) without disturbing the position of your hands, you will find it even more difficult to miss to the left.

Left hand remains over left thigh, thereby maintaining the natural loft on the putter blade.

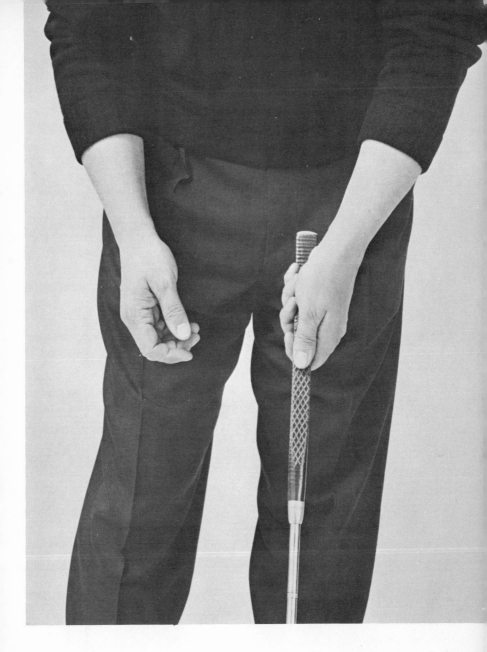

Both hands are slightly to the right of the center of the left thigh.

58

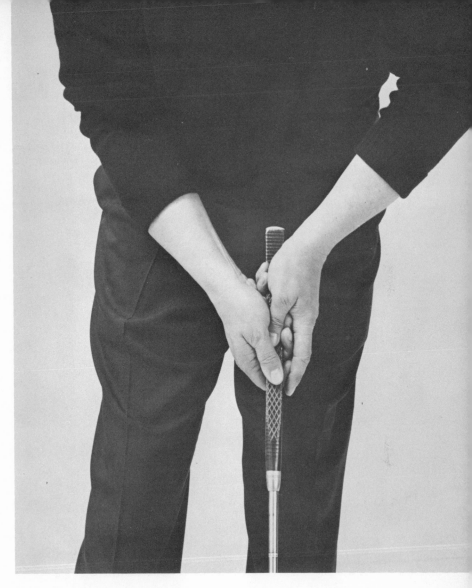

Main pressure on the handle is supplied by the thumb and forefinger of the right hand.

59

Putter is securely locked in a grip that will give you firm-
ness, yet extreme delicacy.

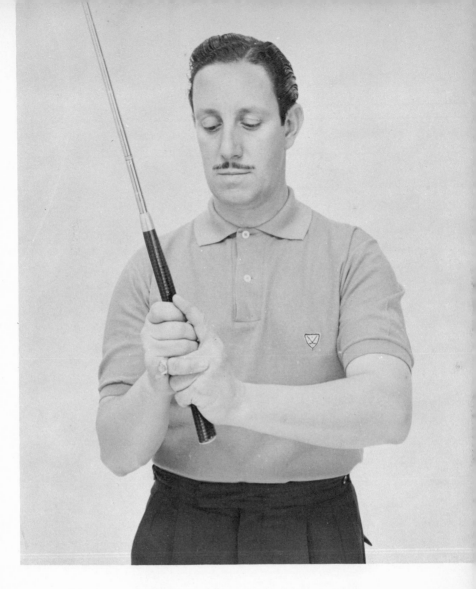

Hands are held at least one inch from end of putter handle.

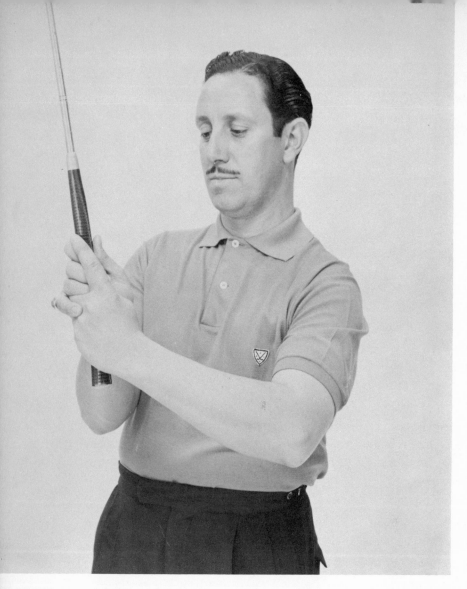

Hands are taking up as little room as possible on the handle of the putter.

You now have your hands locked in a position that is mechanically perfect for accurate putting. Your grip on the putter should be light. The club should be held as lightly as though you were holding a small bird. You wouldn't let it fly away, but then you wouldn't crush it either.

This grip may feel very uncomfortable for a little while. But as you become accustomed to it you will be amazed at the accuracy and delicacy you can acquire in your putting. You are now ready for the basic putting stroke.

The Basic
Putting

IN THE BASIC PUTTING
stroke, the clubhead travels
straight back about four inches
and follows through approximately twelve inches as in the
diagram in this chapter. The actual stroking is done with the
arms, not with the wrists.

Why should you use the arm
rather than the wrist? For this
reason: The object of developing a good basic putting stroke
is to create straight strokes of

Stroke

various lengths with the putter. Let's find out how we best can do this.

Try to draw a straight line with a pencil without moving your forearm, using only your fingers and wrist. You will find that you cannot draw a straight line more than a few inches long. Now try drawing a straight line, not using your wrist but only your arm. You will have no difficulty in drawing a straight line several feet long.

I repeat, the actual stroking is done not with the wrists, but with the arms. The right elbow stays close to the body throughout the stroke, brushing the right side gently as it goes back. If you start your putt back with your fingers or wrists, you may, under tension, close the clubface sharply as

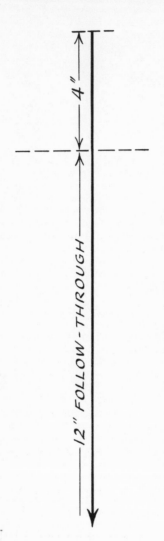

4"

12" FOLLOW-THROUGH

PATH OF THE BASIC PUTTING STROKE

A diagram of this type can be laid out on the floor of your living room for practicing the basic putting stroke.

you stroke the ball, causing a pull to the left. Only when using your arms is it possible to keep the clubface square from the start to the finish of your putting stroke. *The point of energy comes from the right elbow.*

In short, take the club back with the right elbow. *The force that strokes the ball comes from the length of the stroke rather than from the strength applied.*

Practice your basic putting stroke by drawing a diagram similar to the one shown. Start at the point where the solid and dotted lines meet. Take a backswing to the end of the four-inch line and then follow through to the end of the twelve-inch line.

Practice this without a ball until you can follow the diagram quite easily. Then practice your basic putting stroke with a ball. Place the ball where the solid and dotted lines meet in the diagram. (If you put the diagram near a wall or any other solid object, the ball will bounce back to you without your having to retrieve it.) A few minutes of practice each evening for a few evenings will pay big dividends on the putting green.

When you feel that you have your basic putting stroke down pretty well, you are ready to start using a target. You can do this on your own living room rug. Let's use a really small target. Get a needle or a straight pin and stick it through a small piece of white paper, so that you can see it from a distance. Stick the pin, piercing through the paper,

Full backswing of the basic putting stroke. Note the absence of wrist break.

*In the follow-through of the basic putting stroke, the shaft
is in the same relative position to the hands and arms as
it was in the address. The clubhead must never be allowed to get ahead of the left wrist.*

on your living room rug. Then mark off distances of one foot, two feet, three feet, and so on up to six feet. Mark off each foot with a coin or some similar object that will not mar your rug. Then start putting to the pin from the one-foot distance, hitting the pin six consecutive times.

Remember, you must hit the pin with the ball from the one-foot distance six consecutive times. If you get five hits and then a miss, you must start all over again. Only after you have hit the pin six consecutive times should you move back to the two-foot position. You will find the pressure increasing as you hit the fifth and sixth putt.

After you have hit the pin six times in succession from the two-foot position, move back another foot until finally you are able to hit the pin six consecutive times from six feet. When you can do this, you are really putting!

The rewarding part of this exercise is that, once you have mastered it, it is only necessary for you to practice it once a month in order to maintain the putting skill you have acquired. There is no limit to the number of times you may hit the pin. Some of my pupils have worked this up to twelve times from each position.

Now, stop to think. You have been hitting a tiny pin, consistently, from one to six feet! The hole on the golf course is four and a quarter inches in diameter. When you are putting on the green, by comparison the hole will seem as large as a barrel.

By the way, when putting in long sessions, be sure you do not straighten up too fast, or you may pull a muscle in your back. Always get up slowly and you will not hurt yourself.

After you have developed a good degree of accuracy, you are ready to begin judging distances.

Judging

L ET'S FIND OUT, FOR certain, how far your ball will travel with the basic putting stroke. Go onto the practice putting green and stroke a few balls, using the basic putting stroke. Now measure the distance off in feet. You will notice that on a normal green the ball will travel approximately eight feet with the basic putting stroke (that is, with the four-inch backswing and the twelve-

Distance

inch follow-through). If the green is fast, the ball will travel approximately ten feet. A slow green will send the ball about six feet.

Before going out to play, test the practice green to find out how far your basic stroke will send the ball. The rest of the greens will usually be of approximately the same texture and speed. (Remember that the backswing of the basic putting stroke measures only four inches.)

Now, if your ball travels eight feet with the basic four-inch backstroke and you have a sixteen-foot putt, merely go back twice as far (eight inches). The follow-through remains the same. Similarly, as the length of the putt increases, increase the length of your backswing.

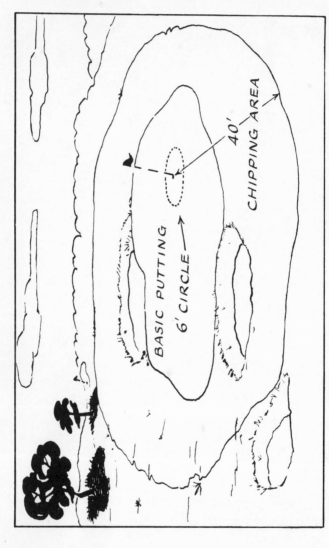

The basic putting circle is your target from six feet out. Once in the six-foot circle, you will be left with a putt of less than three feet.

On the very long putts, play the ball just a little to the right of your left toe so as not to top it. Tee the ball on a line with the right side of your left foot.

Remember, the grass will not remain at the same texture from day to day. Therefore, it is wise to test the practice green before each round. If you haven't the time to go to the practice green, you can test the speed of the greens after you've played out the first hole, provided there is no one waiting behind you to approach the green.

You are not allowed to test the green before playing out the hole. Needless to say, this would annoy your opponent very much, and, besides, the penalty is disqualification.

As you line up your putt, pace from your ball to the hole. (Each step or pace should be approximately three feet long.) Do it casually, so that your opponent will imagine that you are examining your line. If it is a very long putt, just pace halfway and really examine the path your ball must travel over, removing any pebble or foreign matter that is not growing on the green. You have now eliminated a lot of guesswork in your putting.

On the very long putts, visualize a six-foot circle around the hole and putt the ball into that circle, as close to its center as possible. Once in that circle, you will be left with a putt of under three feet. Then you can use your basic putting stroke. By doing so, you will seldom need more than two putts on each green.

Body position at address remains the same in short as well as in long putts.

Note in the long putt the right elbow is still hugging the right side. The left wrist is still unbroken.

Reading the

EADING THE greens is a term that has confused quite a lot of golfers. It merely means being able to figure the line your ball must travel on its way to the hole.

To become a top-rank putter, having perfect mechanics, is a tremendous help. But you must know how to put to use your best putting techniques. It is like having a very fine rifle and

Greens

expecting to hit your target without getting your sights in the proper alignment.

You actually start reading the green well before you get to it. As you are walking up toward the green and you are still approximately a hundred and fifty yards away from it, take a look at it and study it, so that you can see in which direction the entire green is sloping. You can do this best while you are a little distance away from the green. Now, although the green may have many more slopes in it than you can see at a distance, you will have a great advantage while you are putting in knowing and remembering in which direction the entire green slopes.

If you are playing a course near the seashore, the greens

will usually have a tendency to slope toward the ocean. If the course is in a mountainous area, the greens will usually slope away from the mountains. This will be so, even though your naked eye tells you otherwise.

After you have figured the general slope of the green from a distance, your next step, when your ball is on the green, is to figure the line from the ball to the hole. In doing this, your aim is to determine the texture of the grass along that intended line, the distance from the ball to the hole, and the amount of backswing and force needed to get the ball to the hole.

To get the best line from the ball to the hole, stand in back of the ball so that your master eye is doing the aligning. At times it is wise also to line up your putt from the hole to the ball. As you are lining up your putt, ask yourself this question: "If I were to roll a ball with my hand, which path should I take?" You will be amazed at how accurate that alignment will be.

After you have decided your line, then carefully inspect the grass along the line and pick up any specks of dirt that may be in the way. As you walk back from the hole to the ball, remember to count your paces from the hole to the ball casually, to give you some idea of how much backswing to take. Do not be afraid to take all your time surveying your putt— a missed putt is a stroke lost for good.

I repeat, on the very long putts, your aim is to make the

ball stop in the center of that imaginary six-foot circle around the hole, so as to leave yourself a very short putt in case of a miss. At times, there may be a double roll in the line toward the hole. It is advisable to play the roll closest to the hole. A fast-traveling ball will not be affected so much by a slope as will a slow-traveling ball.

The area of the six-foot basic putting circle is where you must be most observant—to the point of examining the direction in which the blades of grass are growing—for they will also affect the roll of the ball. A ball will always break in the direction that the blades of grass are growing. If you have a short, straight putt, you must decide whether to hit the ball a little more firmly or to stroke it gently and allow for the slight break you will get from the direction of the grain, grass, or nap of the green.

The best way to stroke a short putt is to stroke it firmly. A ball that is stroked firmly will hold its line, while a ball that is stroked very softly is left at the mercy of the elements.

Start keeping track of the number of putts you are taking for the eighteen holes; and, after a few rounds of golf, you will be amazed at the number of strokes you are saving. With this system of putting, you will be surprised at how well you will be able to cope with any situation that arises on the green.

The Chip

THE CHIP SHOT IS one of the most important shots in golf. You can hit your drive not quite right, miss the green with your second shot, chip up to the pin for one putt, and still get your par.

The chip shot is the great equalizer in golf. Miss your chip shot and what would have been a par for the hole turns out to be a bogey, or possibly a dou-

Shot

ble bogey. The chip shot is the shot that makes up the difference when a shorter hitter gets up against a long hitter. The short hitter must then depend on his chip shot to get his par, because he lacks the length to reach the long par four holes with his second shot. Whenever the green is missed, it depends upon the chip shot to make par possible.

The chip shot requires the same delicacy and touch that is so necessary in putting. The stroke you use for a long putt is the stroke that you should use for a chip shot. A good putter is usually a good chipper.

Use the same grip for chipping that you are using for putting, with both thumbs on top of the shaft so that the palms of each hand face each other. The reason for this is that the

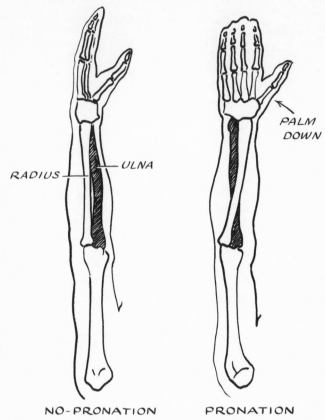

RADIUS — | — ULNA

PALM
DOWN

NO-PRONATION

PRONATION
(RADIUS CROSSES ULNA)

Sketch showing effect on the bones of the forearm when the hand is turned or pronated. The greatest sensitivity of the fingers is attained when the ulna and radius bones are not crossed.

position of the palms affects the two large bones in the forearm called the ulna and the radius bones. When the palms are faced downward, these two bones cross each other, giving the golfer less delicacy in his touch. When the ulna and radius bones are not crossed, there is a greater sensitivity in the hands.

In chipping we need all the touch and feel of which we are capable. The arms and hands do all the work—that is why the position of the hands is so vital.

The stance is square as it is in the putt, with the feet just a little farther apart. The body weight is mostly on the left foot and toward the heels. Body movement in a chip shot is at a minimum.

The only difference between a long putt and a chip shot is the choice of club and the longer backswing and follow-through. The maximum backswing for a chip shot is reached when your club shaft is horizontal to the ground, the follow-through being equal.

The target for the chip shot is the same as in putting. You chip for the imaginary circle, six feet in diameter, around the hole. Once in that circle, you are left with a basic putt of less than three feet, making it quite possible to get down in one putt. You will even be surprised to see quite a few chip shots go into the cup.

I know you are quite anxious to find out which club to use in chipping; so let's go down to the practice green, tak-

The Chip Shot: *The stance is the same as in the putt, except that the ball is played just off the right side of the left foot. This brings your ball to the bottom of the stroking arc, thereby eliminating topping.*

The Quarter Chip Shot: *Used for short distances.*

The Half Chip Shot: *Note left wrist beginning to straighten out slightly.*

The Full Chip Shot: *Note right wrist is almost straight. There is a minimum of body movement. The knees are still facing straight ahead. Body weight is still on left.*

Follow-through for the short chip shot. The clubhead must not be permitted to get ahead of the left wrist. Left elbow still points out, but is raised.

Follow-through for full chip shot. Again, clubhead should not be permitted to get ahead of the left wrist.

In some instances the ball can be chipped out of the sand. Only when the lie is clean, the same stroke is used as on the apron of the green. Remember, do not sole club while addressing the ball in the sand, since it is a penalty.

ing your 7-, 8-, and 9-irons with you. Now, while you are on the apron of the green, take your 9-iron and a few practice balls and chip a few balls onto the green, using the putting stroke. Remember to play the ball just a little to the right of the left toe, in line with the right side of your left foot.

Take a few full chip shots with your 9-iron. Also remember that, in a full chip shot, the clubhead goes back about waist high up to the point where the shaft of your club is level or horizontal to the ground. The follow-through will be equally as long. The energy that strokes the ball comes from the size of the circle rather than from the force supplied.

After you have taken about a dozen full chip shots, you will notice that the balls are bunched at approximately the same distance away from where you were chipping. Now start pacing off from where you were chipping to the center of the group of balls. You will find that the average distance that the ball traveled was approximately forty paces. Now, if a full chip with a 9-iron travels forty paces, a half chip shot will travel half that distance: twenty paces. If, in a full chip shot, the clubhead goes back to the point where the shaft of the club is horizontal to the ground, in a half chip shot the clubhead will go back half the distance of a full chip shot, halfway between the horizontal point and the ground. A quarter chip shot, in turn, will go back only half the distance of a half chip shot. And so, if a full chip shot with a 9-iron will send the ball approximately forty paces or forty yards and a half chip shot, also with the 9-iron, will send the ball about twenty paces or twenty yards, then a quarter chip shot will send the ball about ten paces, and so forth.

A full chip shot with an 8-iron will travel about five paces more than with a 9-iron: approximately forty-five paces. A full chip shot with a 7-iron will send the ball still another five paces: approximately fifty paces.

Your key club in chipping is your 9-iron. Under normal conditions, it should be used for anything up to forty paces, although almost any iron can be used successfully in chipping. The great advantage in chipping with your 9-iron is that the ball can be stroked more firmly. Therefore, it will cover most of the distance in the air and will not be influenced by a bad bounce off the apron of the green.

Strive to make your ball land on the green on its first bounce. With a lofted club like the 9-iron, you can do this without fear of running too far past the hole. You can chip right for the pin; for a 9-iron will give the ball a slight degree of backspin. You will also find this especially useful when going over a trap or a bunker.

When more loft and backspin are needed, a chip with your wedge will make the ball stop even more quickly. At times, when the lie is good and the trap shallow, a chip out of the trap with your 9-iron will produce amazing results.

You have now eliminated quite a lot of guesswork in

your putting and chipping. Just a little practice will enable you to get down in two from any distance up to fifty yards. A little time spent in practicing this putting and chipping method will be rewarded by less wastage of strokes and lower scores.

Bi-monthly Practice

THE FOLLOWING pages describe a rather specific routine to improve the putting and chipping techniques you have learned in this book. By devoting one morning of extensive practice to these "exercises" you will exhibit marked improvement in your game for approximately two months. Spend approximately four hours on your putting and chipping drills to insure satisfactory results.

Routine

Putting

LET'S BEGIN with putting practice. Remember to incorporate the suggestions that I have offered. And, above all, try to make these incorporations unconscious reactions. Try to get to the point where you can do them without thinking about them—do them as if you've been doing them all your life.

On a practice putting green, draw an imaginary circle around the cup, at a radius of one foot from the cup. Using this one-foot putt as the starting point, place balls at various points around the circle and practice sinking them until you can sink six consecutive putts from this distance.

Now expand your imaginary circle until it has a two-foot radius. Again, with the balls placed around the circumference of the circle, practice putting until you sink six consecutively from the two-foot mark.

Continue to expand your circle to three feet, four, five, and finally six feet. Remember, you must sink six balls consecutively from each distance before going on to the next distance. You are only cheating yourself if you move farther out without sinking all the balls.

Now you are ready to attempt longer putts.

Make a three-foot jump in the radius of your imaginary circle to nine feet and attempt several putts (about fifteen or twenty) from this distance. Your object from the longer distances will be to putt as close to the cup as possible, not to sink any consecutive number. After you have become fairly proficient from nine feet, move to twelve feet, then fifteen, and finally eighteen—in each case, attempting to get as close as possible.

This simple drill, with the aids offered in other parts of the book, will enable you to cut many putting strokes off your total score. You will be amazed at how your score will drop.

Chipping

LET'S CONCENTRATE on your chip shot. Again, I urge you to incorporate all the techniques and pointers you've learned earlier in this book. If you learn these pointers until they become habits, chipping will come very easily.

Begin your chip shot drill about three yards from the pin. With your 9-iron, chip at least two dozen balls. Continue chipping until you are able to place all the balls within a one-putt area of the pin.

Now move out another three yards. You are now six yards out. Still using your 9-iron, practice chipping until you can place two dozen balls within a one-putt area of the pin. This one-putt area is determined by your ability to sink putts consistently from a particular distance.

Continue to move out at three-yard intervals, chipping to the one-putt area with your 9-iron. When you have reached your maximum chipping distance with the 9-iron, switch to the 8-iron, and continue with the same idea in mind—to get within a one-putt area of the pin.

Practice chipping with the 8-iron by moving out at three-yard intervals until you have reached a maximum distance. Then, change to your 7-iron, always attempting to place each ball within a one-putt distance of the pin. Once more, move out until you have reached the maximum distance for the 7-iron.

Consistency is what you should strive for in all golf drills, and in your every movement on the links. Keeping this in mind, along with the learning process in which you practice until your movements become unconscious reactions, you can clip many strokes off your score and enjoy your game more and more with each new round.